Love Poems for Peace

The Poetry of
Iyana Ife Jendeyea Davis
b.k.a.
YaNi

Love Poems for Peace

For information, www.whoisyani.com

Book & Cover Design by Tiffany Stubbs, Dezign Dogma, LLC
www.dezigndogma.com

ISBN-10: 0-9915448-0-3

First Edition: February 2014

Dedicated to The Creator, The one True Spirit that allows inspiration and creativity to flow from my mind to your eyes, hearts and ears.

To the parents that Created me. The ones who took the time to nurture my budding mind, my love for words and my life-long quest to be a vessel of peace, transformation and love. The two that became one and instructed me to "Lead the People in Love."

To my spiritual parent, who acknowledged me as "Her Dream" and the dream of the ancestors. The one who walked me to this side of awareness and continues to pray that the fullness of all I am liberates the masses.

Table of Contents

Forward

Love Poems for Peace was written with one person in mind: the person who believes it's not too late to change the world! Much of our hope for a better future has left and it is up to us, The Peace People, to bring it back.

As you read this book, remember the lover, the fighter, and all the Peace within you so you can be encouraged to keep dreaming and living. For many of the poems peace is personified as the only way we can get to a more juste world. For some of the poems, my heart was hurting and I needed to vent. For all of the poems, I had triumph in love and triumph in life in mind. I hope you enjoy and always remember to Be Peace, Know Peace and Live Peace.

Sincerely Yours,
YaNi

Wholeness

Inspired by the self I forgot about

The one that died to ego and rose again in wholeness

I am the epitome of wellness springing in a soul full of joy

Once abandoned, once forgotten

Inspiration brought me back to a place of

Oneness and clarity... my only friends in a world of

Pain, pointlessness and poverty

Where I come from, poor is a disease and rich means quite alright

Where I am, peace is power and materials mean nothing

Meet me here and see how internal wealth overflows from

The hearts and mouths of those who get it

Those who dare to never let it go

This space isn't just safe

It's all I've lived for and imagined

Make me over and make me new

Show me the depths of this self

The depths of this 4-letter-L-word

That is and was the essence of all I am

We are the ones that waited for ourselves

No one else was going to think about us or save us

Or look at us or dare to understand us

You are here

You look good...

Now keep going

peace is power
and materials
mean nothing

-YaNi

Still?

Peace told me to be still

But peace is the very reason I can't

I was caught between hating me and loving more

And the love part won

Won me over and put me in the position to never go back

I wanted to return to those lazy ways

Non-committed, shadowed behind dislike and hate

How far have we gone from knowing the truth

Verses being the truth?

I'm convinced ain't no more lies to tell

At least lies we haven't heard before

I am proof that change happens when change comes

And here I am, different than before.

I am the epitome of
wellness springing up
in a soul full of joy

-YaNi

Heart - Work

The heart work goes so deep

I forgot to ask if it was okay to love you

How dare we walk around blind to

I mean dead to, or is it unaware of

Your fiery goodness

I was caught, until you spread.

Wild, free, inevitable

I've imagined this moment, where,

Pure hope and my un-fathomable

Destiny combine and mean more than the depths of my knowledge

I know you are near

I know you are mine

The heart work was the hard part

Now I celebrate the birth day of

My liberation and my introduction to you

It's heart work.

The heart work was
the hard part

-YaNi

Creator

My heart beat is much slower when I write songs for you.

I feel you moving ever so beautifully through me

Life isn't a maze it's a journey and with you I travel well

I pack light like and I wrote words that fill your people with joy

I guess I'm the baby bear and you're the poppa bear

making sure my porridge is just right

Creation is just a reflection of you and I'm a reflection of it.

I feel you moving
ever so beautifully
through me

-YaNi

Vessels

Songs didn't sum up the power in my voice

Overtaken by the beat and the drum and the melody

Melancholy me, wrote it right but never heard what I was saying

The music moves me, loosely,

But the words stir my core

So I wrote this for all of you

The you's that will never receive anything more

I wrote this for all of us

The us's who need more than a selfie to feel our self-worth

I wrote this for them

The them's that think our society is post-racial

I wrote it for the light-seekers

Because darkness was confusing

And hope was all I had left

I wrote it for the children

Because they need to know we love them

They need to know there's a better way and

The revolution won't be tweeted or put in a rap song

The revolution is in your mind little one, and your heart

Have you stopped to feel it?

The music
moves me,
loosely,
But the words
stir my core

-YaNi

Movement I

The rhythm was right,

Right enough to get my two left feet going

My arms similarly, joined in on the fun

Or was it work because I was moving

But the movement wasn't enough to fix the mess

The last generation didn't dance enough and this one,

They dance too much. So I'm stuck in the middle

With no one, attempting to bring them all together

For the better of course, Soul and Pop

Hip Hop and Bee Bop

Rock and Folk for the folk who need it the most

Generations of be-ers and see-ers

Guess it's time for us to move as one

Til the moving is done and the question isn't

Are we equal..the question then will be..

Are we all still moving?

Guess it's time
for us to
move as one

-YaNi

thoughtLESS

The blank pages were making me sick

And polluting the current age…

All different ages misguided by who they thought were leaders

The teachers were afraid to lose their jobs

So each age was given the same garbage

The garbage produced more garbage and minds

Were left mind-less and less and less

People thought only about what they were instructed to think about

So thought was no longer thought, just instruction

No need to discuss destruction because in the minds of the masses

It was just garbage anyway

Cast down, forgotten about, abandoned

Just like me.

The blank pages were
making me sick

-YaNi

Appreciation

Good mourning sunshine ain't seen you in a minute

Looking at the grass and decided to sit in it

Cause it's been a while since I appreciated life.

Everything considered wrong, all the things I'm doing right

Write it down make it plain, sometimes my vision gets blurry

Grandma told me haste makes waste don't do it in a hurry

So I'm taking a moment to thank god for the blessin'

Heaven on earth hurt like hell

I'm thankful for the lesson

Cause who I am now could never relive the past

My joy met me this morning so the sorrow never lasts.

Heaven on earth
hurt like hell

-YaNi

A-gain

Hearts shattered

More like glass than valves and vessels

Poignant,

Displaced

Erased

I fall to the ground in utter turmoil

No forgiveness for the one who could never quite get it right

Tomorrow will be better

No more forever

The pieces are all that's left.

Tomorrow
will be better

-YaNi

Children

Dear God, what's up with my soul?

Got me thinking about staying young and growing old

Cause there's no country for old people and there's no space for a child that

doesn't have its own

Some days I don't feel like God blessed Me

I just feel like God left me

Cause they're worshiping Jesus and praising themselves

All they care about is the stuff on these shelves

Not the heart inside or the power they possess

So I write their stories and I tell them

Because everyone who transitioned and now I transition into

A healer through words a mouthpiece for

Jesus children, Jesus children

Jesus children don't you get he wasn't just a savior he showed you how to save

yourself

Healing is a choice, do you feel it?

Better yet can you think it?

Don't let the thought be fleeting let wholeness be more than a word

Let it be your world

So I'm telling my story of growing up hurt

And what I had inside was the light

That led me to truth

God I know what's up with my soul now

I'm not afraid and they don't like that

Freedom should be granted

But every day I live to demand it

So a child born tomorrow doesn't have to.

I just feel like
God left me

-YaNi

I-Am

I am the heart.

Beat of a world that has lost its way

I am the vessel by which children learn to grow deeper and wiser

I am the light that most have forgotten about

I am the Source, divinely guided, clothed in flesh

And you are the same

Made in the image of a God that loved me so much

That I was granted a chance to roam the earth

Roam the passageways that lead to liberation and enlightenment

I am the heart.

Beating-fast because I hear transformation

And I just can't get enough

I am the vessel
by which children
learn to grow
deeper and wiser

-YaNi

Slow Down

Angels are flying or walking next to me

I feel them…

swoop past me sometimes

When I'm forced to slow down,

That is them holding me still

Released, to love on me for a little while longer

I wrote a song for her and him because

They carry inspiration from God's heart to my ears

And my fingers tend to write the words down

So thank you earth angels for your love

And inspiration,

Because after all inspiration is simply God's way of telling me,

I'm still here.

They carry
inspiration from
God's heart
to my ears

-YaNi

Deferred

You caught me, Love

I didn't know what to say or do with you

I just kinda looked at you and wondered what it meant to have what

I always wanted

A companion, a friend, someone to help carry the load

My mind couldn't fathom the realness of you

The feel of you was what was most alarming

Warm and fuzzy insides mixed with baby elephant feet walking around

My mind is the place that dreamt of you

My heart is now catching up

When I've been without you so long

I forgot how to treat you

I forgot how to be with you

I forgot how to make love with you

So, I'll have to leave you.

I didn't know
what to say
or do
with you

-YaNi

Front

Isn't that the way it goes every time?

Love and Left to wait for the right time

Or the right one

What if anyone is the right one

That'd mean love could be love

And love would be love without anyone interfering

Longevity in love is about taking notes

About your lover and your love for others

And love's love for love

The wrong one, right time

Who's ready now?

Please step to the front of the line.

Who's ready now?

-YaNi

Soul-Work

Broke my heart in two weeks flat

Guess karma ain't done with me yet

Imagined a life with you within an hour of meeting

Showed you my scars til they magically healed themselves

Showed you my heart once I took it down from the shelf

And well my soul couldn't hide from the magnetism I felt

the second you looked into my eyes

Guess love is more than the time it takes to cook honesty up real good

Cause now you're gone and all I have is me.

Guess karma ain't
done with me yet

-YaNi

EX-CAVATED

You took it and I don't even think you stopped to think how much it hurt

First day I met you, I knew

I knew you'd be the one to take the syrupy sweet out of my honey

I knew you'd drain the love out of my most hidden parts

Not the outwardly physical ones

The spiritual ones

That is where you dwell

Because excavation never worked well with matters of these parts

Matters of a heart that was only hypothetical

Never tangible

But it's okay.

You took it.

Love, you took my peace.

Love,
you took
my peace.

-YaNi

You

I'll

Take you

I mean

Us

I mean

I'll have us

We will do.

We will do.

-YaNi

Gone

My heart longs for you

Moments past when balance was maintained

I wait in the doorway considering entrance back into chaos

But solitude was sweet and necessary

Time to create time and precious memories I've only imagined

Imagine us, walking hand in hand....again

Laying in the greeny, blue grass we had grown to love

It would prick us when we'd lose touch with reality

But also serve as the magic carpet that escorted us to outter limits

I rang the bell but know-one came to my rescue

Daylight wouldn't even shine on my somber face

You are the calm to mercury

You are the god and the star Venus

You are all I imagined you to be

But you are not present.

And you are no more

Imagine us,
walking
hand in hand
...again

-YaNi

Pieces

You lie there

And see no problem with it

Never stopping to think,

Perhaps I need all of you.

Perhaps the parts of me that are in love with you

Don't need Convincing just Conversation

A simple word

A gentle whisper in an ear that has been burning for ages

Why won't you get up?

Perhaps I need
all of you?

-YaNi

Depths

Silence,

I accept you and thank you for showing me where

Love is.

Just sitting with you is enough to take me to deeper depths

The deeper I grow, the farther you show me

The more my destiny makes sense

The less the world does

Perhaps I am a bit confused

My experience as a creature of light

Reveal to me the power of darkness

The chaos created there and then

There's you,

Waiting for me patiently on the other side

How dare I run to anything or anyone but you

How dare I escape the pastures of a love that is.

Loyalty, Light, Living and Free.

Silence, I get you and I embrace you,

For you have lead me to love and your ways don't scare me anymore

Internally Resting, Experientially Awake, More Vibrant than I was before.

Silence,
I accept you
and thank you
for showing me
where Love is

-YaNi

Hope-FULL

You're my hope for a new day

You're my refuge when others won't stay

My heart needs to heal my soul needs to feel the power of love once again

How is it the lesson hasn't been learned

Over again stripes haven't been earned

My high feels low my low is underground

My self is off wandering and can not be found

The line never finished the score never appeared

Calls from the wrong ones, The debt never cleared

I gave all I could.

Restore me.

Restore me.

-YaNi

Questioning

What if I told you I wanted you,

What if I said I needed you ?

How about I'd never let you go?

Squeeze you so tight,

You'd come oozing out of me

        onto

Every single person

Looking and longing for more of you.

Hey there, Nice to meet you.

How about,
I'd never
let you go?

-YaNi

Humanity

Sweet humanity where did your love go?

Instant sanity the ebb and glow

When my mind can't escape it and my heart can't take it

I call sweet humanity to carry me home.

Sweet humanity,
where did
your love go?

-YaNi

Moving II

Emotional me, Emotionally waits in the hidden passages of your mind

As fear overtakes my spine, I cannot move

It's hard living here without you

Why'd you leave?

The cold wisps through my body and I forget the

Feelings I once had.

Emotional me, Emotionally waits in the hidden passages of your mind

As fear overtakes my spine and I cannot move

The question was, where are you?

Are we still moving?

Or are you moving in the direction of another

Shrinking back never produces the outcome we want

And well, you were just the beat.

The beat I needed to break on

The beat that going on and on and on...

Emotional me. Emotionally.

Cannot move.

Are we still moving?

-YaNi

Moving III

My feet are tired but nowhere near as tired as

The Elders, the ones with wisdom

They fought so you could manifest your dreams in a world like this

Seems forces of darkness and light don't play fair

But pick and choose when it's their turn to shine

So I only pray to be as faithful as the one's who walked

And the ones who hid in the passageways between

Freedom and forever captivity

Did you forget them? Did you leave them?

Subjecting them to Post-Traumatic trances

That leave us all still.

Still, I work for the movement and un-

stuck what you so politely forgot about.

There is another way....

Still.

There is
another
way.....

-YaNi

Gone II

Surely Goodness and Mercy shall follow me

They said blessings chase the righteous

They told me I was more than a conqueror

But what happens when the Sister Warrior

Is left to fight alone?

Where does she go when humanity has left the sight

of the scene and everyone chooses to flee

immediately to the den of insanity and forgiveness

Some days, anger takes over as solitude

Yields soliloquies dedicated to fallen soldiers

The ones who Keep Forgettin' the them's that hate us

But what happens
when the
Sister Warrior
Is left to
fight alone?

-YaNi

Regret

What are you thinking about?

Hurt by the silence that is or

Was.

BEGGING the gods of peace to remove this

Rest-less-ness

Nestled in the middle of my chest.

Sometimes, it moves to the pit of my belly

Hard

To digest spiritual food.

The kind that only the thinkers know about

I recall our precious moments,

The ones that didn't die but

Live on in the part of my brain that is life-giving

Where are you??

I need you

I lost u(s)

What was I thinking?

Hurt by the silence
that is or
Was.

-YaNi

AFTER+ALL

The night,

When alone,

I crave

What I've never had

Only the thought is enough

To bring my heart back to where it should be

I am not the absence of life but fully present in every moment

I imagine you changed how I used to be

I don't regret the shift.

I regret not being able to take more with me

More on this journey to freedom

It feels good on this side

Living and loving and all that.

I don't
regret
the shift

-YaNi

ENOUGH

The desire never leaves

I suffer

Waiting for the day when changes are truly made

Different doesn't make it better

Just opens up the door for potential

And more desire

More longing for what could be

What used to be

What may be

Prayers of the righteous

The soul of a servant

An act of The Almighty

Still, more longing and desire.

I suffer

-YaNi

BE-LONGING

The intangible became real the day you reappeared

Magic was no longer magic

It was just us.

Real as my existence the day I was reborn

Birthed into a world that doesn't understand me

Born into a captive place where security can only be found

At a dinner table playing an innocent game of footsie

And glancing at you glancing at me

We tried our attempt at subtle but our stare was too loud

Our whispers echoed and our silent hearts pounded,

Against the pavement we etched L and P

Because our initials didn't stand for us

Merely bodies, drawn together

Minds drawn together.

Hearts like ours belong together.

It was
just us.

-YaNi

ANCESTRIAL

I submit my life as a living sacrifice because being acceptable to God means more than the flesh he's given me.

I stand in awe of the Creator that sent a sacrifice for the masses that refuse to listen..

They refuse to love, refuse to give, refuse to be born....again. We refuse to live.

I submit my life to the one true god who sent the ancestors as examples of the work we are to do

How dare we say we're lost when the God who sits high and looks low sent example after example of what our lives are to look like

The prince of peace the one who showed us how to be here and submit to gods will

Never did he complain never did he whine about a life dedicated to service

The spirit made flesh is the only way my son sick soul could be made whole

So I cry out..make me an instrument of your peace.

I will continue to use these vessels and this vessel

As streams of life and light flowing through me and to you

I'll use these neurons as energy to give hope to those crying in the middle of the night

I will use the breath of life to flow into and around the children whose parents don't get them and don't accept them and don't love them and hug them and appreciate them.

Ill submit this life as a sacrifice because mortality doesn't scare me

Not fulfilling my purpose does.

God hasn't forsaken us we've forsaken Her.

Make me an Instrument of thy peace so I can play and think and write and be like you

Make me an instrument of your peace so I can walk and talk and live like you

Make me an instrument of your peace so I can be used and renewed by you

Make me an instrument of you peace so I can spread peace like you

So I can flow like you so I can grow like you

Be bold like you

Make me an instrument of your peace so I can experience a piece of you.

Make me an instrument of your peace so I can cry like you and try like you and one day die in the name of peace, love, justice and sacrifice like you.

God hasn't
forsaken us,
we've forsaken
Her.

-YaNi

ShE

Feminine energy spoke to me

Said the world won't make it without me

Swooped into the hearts and minds of the People

Strength no longer meant power but it meant

Progress. I stretched my arms toward her

Embraced her and said,

Now we can complete what we set out to do.

Now we can complete what we set out to do.

-YaNi

Heaven

Love sent from a place we can only think of

Proudest day of the life of a life-giver

We believe in the hope they had for us

Thoughts weren't enough to keep the bloodline going and that good love flowing

Blessed beyond measure to enter the world

And you were the vessel I came into being through

My breath of life, my memory of the womb, my heart beat

All come from…You!

I honor the day you let me loose because the world was ever changed

because of it

Thank you would not be enough so I just say Amen.

As the days continue to pass, as the nights continue to fade to morning

We remember the life of the one who stood tall and made a creation so special

It is this, The Gift of Life that makes this moment so special

It's time to celebrate..a mom..a daughter and a daughter's daughter as Love

continues to give life once more.

Thank you
would not be
enough
so I just say
Amen.

-YaNi

NAMESAKE

Peace, I love you

No space, no time

Just the yellows and silent blues

High-low.

You are my inspiration

You are the reason I smile

You are the thought that strikes the nerve memory

That shoots to the corners of my mouth

And the middle of my cheeks

You, the very reason outside forces no longer move

The unshakeable

And I am the light behind your glow

Your reason for radiating

The warm open embrace that holds tight

Never smothers: Just enough for me to get by

Just enough to go beyond..just enough to pass go and

Keep going

Peace, I thank you, for without you…

None of this would have been possible.

Peace,
I love you.

-YaNi

Made in the USA
Columbia, SC
22 December 2022

73604728R00043